GROSS LIMERICKS!!!

A young man whose sight was myopic
Shied away from all sex, as a topic.
 So poor were his eyes
 That despite its great size
His member appeared microscopic.

A Russian young lady of fashion,
Had oodles and oodles of passion.
 To her lovers she said,
 As they'd climb into bed,
"Here's one thing those Commies can't ration!"

There was a young lady from Plain View
Whose boyfriend said, "May I explore you?"
 She replied to the chap,
 "No, I'll draw you a map,
Where others have been to before you."

GROSS
LIMERICKS

By Julius Alvin

ZEBRA BOOKS
KENSINGTON PUBLISHING CORP.

To the Superbas
In hopes of a gross of victories in 1984.

CONTENTS

1

INDECENT RELIGIOUS LIMERICKS

The frustrated priest, Father Lou
Found a novice young nun who would screw.
    But he hadn't the knack,
    And thrust too far back.
She said, "Father, you're in the wrong pew!"

A young nun in theology class,
Preferred screwing to going to Mass.
    Her lust was so great,
    That by quarter past eight,
Her habit was covered by grass.

———————

'Twas a hardened old Biblical fossil.
Though a find, it seemed hardly colossal.
    But the Vatican thought,
    From the wonders it wrought,
'Twas the peter of Paul the apostle.

"When I see a monk's ass, I just grab it,"
Said a lazily amorous abbot.
"Though it's vastly more fun,
To make love to a nun,
It's so hard to get into the habit."

———————————

There was a young nun of Gibraltar
Who was raped by a priest at the altar.
It really seems odd
That a servant of God
Should answer her prayers and assault her.

A nun and a priest from Hoboken
Were shipwrecked while sailing the ocean.
    In eighty-one days,
    They had sex eighty ways.
Imagine such fucking devotion!

The pretty nun's life was so bleak
That she taught her vagina to speak.
    It was frequently liable
    To quote from the Bible
But cursed when she was taking a leak.

There was a young lady from Chichester,
Who made all the saints in their niches stir.
    One morning at matins,
    Her breasts in white satins,
Made the Bishop of Chichester's britches stir.

———————

There was a young girl from Cape Cod,
Who thought babies were fashioned by God.
    But it was not the Almighty,
    Who lifted her nightie,
It was Roger, the lodger, by God.

The priest was seduced by a siren,
But his cock was the size of a pin.
    Said the whore, with a laugh
    As she touched his short shaft,
"This fuck won't be much of a sin."

A Bishop whose see was Vermont,
Used to jerk himself off in the font.
    The baptistry stank
    With an odor so rank
That no one would sit up in front.

A flatulent nun of Hawaii
One Christmas eve supped on papaya.
    Then on the very next day,
    She offered to play
With her ass, the whole Handel's Messiah.

———————————

A synod of Catholic friars,
Were discussing their carnal desires.
    Said a priest, sipping tea,
    "No fat nuns are for me.
It's a slim altar boy that inspires."

I sat next to the preacher at tea.
It was just as I feared it would be.
    His emissions abdominal
    Were simple abominable,
And everyone thought it was me!

———————

In all of the Grecian metropolis
There was only one virgin—Papapoulis;
    But her cunt was all callous
    From fucking a phallus
Of a god that adorned the Acropolis.

A sequestered nun in the convent,
With a candle her passions did vent.
    Night out and night in,
    She lay writhing in sin,
Giving thanks it was ten months to Lent.

———————————

From the depths of the crypt at St. Giles
Came a scream that resounded for miles.
    Said the abbot, "My word!
    Has Father Stoddard,
Forgotten the Bishop has piles?"

2

FOUL HOMOSEXUAL LIMERICKS

To Christopher Street came a guy
Who was hetero, homo and bi.
    He could have or be had
    By a lass or a lad
Or even by both when he'd try.

Said a beefy old bull dyke named Fawn,
"A dildo is really a con.
    But it's less of a joke,
    If I'm drunk when I poke,
Which is why I keep tying one on."

Said Jane, to her mother, "I fear,
My husband's turned into a queer.
    On Sundays and Mondays
    He irons my undies,
And he secretly wears my brassiere."

"Since my sex is bisex," said Casey,
"I've chosen a city that's racy.
    With its either-or zest,
    I get letters addressed,
To WASHINGTON, D.C. AND A.C."

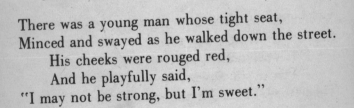

There was a young man whose tight seat,
Minced and swayed as he walked down the street.
    His cheeks were rouged red,
    And he playfully said,
"I may not be strong, but I'm sweet."

There was a strange fellow named Rice
Whose sex life was colder than ice,
    Till a male relation
    Restored his sensation,
Showing him homosexual vice.

———————————

A woman who lived in Tucksberry,
Suspected her son was a fairy.
    "It's peculiar," said she,
    "For he sits down to pee,
Then stands when I bathe my dog Harry."

A sensitive fellow named Harry
Thought sex too revolting to marry.
    So he frowned on the girls,
    Wore dresses and curls,
And he got to be known as a fairy.

———————————

There was a sad wife down in Kent
Whose old man, his pecker was bent.
    She said, with a sigh,
    "Oh, why must it die?
Let's fill it with rubber cement."

There was an old fag name of Bruce
Who won a young boy by a ruse.
 He filled up his rear fusilage
  With a strong brand of mucilage
And he never could pry himself loose.

———————

There was a young man of Australia
Who painted his ass like a dahlia.
 The drawing was fine,
  The color divine,
The scent—ah, that was a failure.

There was a young Sappho named Anna
Who stuffed her friend's cunt with banana
    Which she sucked bit by bit
    From her partner's warm slit
In the most approved lesbian manner.

———————

Said the mythical King of Algiers
To his harem assembled, "My dears,
    You may think it odd of me,
    But I'm tired of sodomy,
Tonight there'll be fucking!" (Loud cheers)

A gay steward who sailed on a clipper,
Was quite a perverted young nipper.
    He plugged up his ass,
    With fragments of glass,
And circumcised the skipper.

———————————

A winsome young fairy from Crete,
Sold his body to tars in the street.
    He went sailing one day,
    And in a most casual way,
He clapped up the whole Turkish fleet.

There was an old mucker named Price,
Who practiced every manner of vice.
    He had cripples and boys,
    And mechanical toys,
And on Sundays, he diddled with mice.

———————

There was a young Turkish cadet,
Who won a remarkable bet,
    For his tool was so long,
    And incredibly strong,
That he buggered six Greeks en brochette.

Two fussy old queers from Algiers
Were flustered and almost in tears,
    For the buggers had spent
    What they needed for rent,
And their landlord had said, "No arrears."

Two dykes from the far Adriatic,
Deciding to be more pragmatic,
    Have switched from mere handling,
    To mutual candling.
The result is, they're waxing ecstatic.

Lisped a limp-wristed cowboy named Ray,
"It's a hell of a place to be gay.
    I must, on these prairies,
    For shortage of fairies,
With the deer and the antelope play."

———————

There once was a horny Norwegian
Who enlivened the French Foreign Legion.
    But his brothers-in-arms
    Who succumbed to his charms
Got syphillis in their rear regions.

The young man was hardly a prude.
He posed for artists in the nude.
    But he drew the line
    When fags touched his behind
And decided it ought to be screwed.

———————

A charming young gay guy named Bruce,
Whose favorite thrill was a goose,
    At the touch of a thumb
    He could feel himself come
And his bowels got all tingly—and loose.

A gay prostitute name of Rick
Picked up old drag queens as tricks.
    With his hands on their hips
    He'd apply his hot lips
To their nipples and testes and pricks.

———————

The hottest sex book in the writing
Was a treatise on cunts and their sucking.
    But in Frisco this work
    Was eclipsed by a Turk
Whose book was on assholes and their fucking.

There once were two brothers named Luntz
Who buggered each other at once.
    Then asked to account
    For this intricate mount
They said, "Assholes are tighter than cunts."

———————

A young man who lacked an alliance
Began fucking his own ass, in defiance
    Not only of custom,
    And morals, God bless 'em,
But most of the known laws of science.

A man was approached by a queer,
Who made his intentions quite clear.
    The man said, "I'm no prude,
    So don't think me rude,
But I hate having pricks in my rear."

———————

A gay traveler in Khartoum
Found a lesbian bunked in his room.
    They argued for nights
    Over who had the right
To do what, and with which, to whom.

The gays that the faggot was bedding
Were stunned when asked to his wedding.
    But he's married a lass
    With a face like an ass
And a passion for fellatiating.

———————————

There was a young faggot named Lloyd
Whose rear end was studded with hemorrhoids.
    They ticked so nice
    That he drew a high price
From the other gay feminine boys.

A bisexual chap name of Lunt
Taught himself an unusual stunt.
    He could peel back his spout,
    Then turn the skin inside out
Like a glove, to be used as a cunt.

———————————

King Louis gave a lesson in class,
Simultaneously screwing a lass.
    When she used the word, "Damn,"
    He rebuked her, "Please, ma'am,
Keep a more civil tongue up my ass."

Well screwed was a boy named DuPlasse,
By all of the lads in his class.
    Then he said, with a yawn,
    "Now the novelty's gone,
And love's only a pain in the ass."

———————————

There once was a warden at Wadham,
Who approved of the customs of Sodom.
    "For a man might," he said,
    "Have a very poor head,
But be a fine fellow at bottom."

3

VULGAR CRIPPLE LIMERICKS

There was a young lady named Glitch
Who for sadism had a strong itch.
    In her box she put pepper,
    And slept with a leper,
And castrated the fellow, the bitch!

The young man received a great jar,
When his cock was shot off in the war.
    So he painted his front
    To resemble a cunt,
And set himself up as a whore.

———————

There was a rich woman named Hyatt
Who screwed a big man on the quiet.
    But down by the wharf,
    She'd visit a dwarf,
Whenever she went on a diet.

A reckless punk rocker named Tate,
Got drunk before tying on skates.
    But he fell on his cutlass
    Which rendered him nutless,
And practically useless on dates.

———————

In the harem, a lonely girl calls,
But the guard, all-unheeding, just sprawls.
    When he's asked if he cheats,
    On the sultan, he bleats,
"Oh, I would—but I haven't the balls."

There was a young man name of Paul,
Whose cock was exceedingly small.
    So he had the habit,
    Of screwing with rabbits,
But the hares scarcely felt it at all.

———————

There was a young man of Nantucket
Whose prick was so long, he could suck it.
    He said with a grin,
    As he wiped off his chin,
"If my ear were a cunt, I could fuck it."

There was a young woman named Brent
With a cunt of enormous extent.
    And so deep and so wide
    The acoustics inside
Were so good you could hear when you spent.

———————

A winsome young lass name of Blount
Was cursed with a rectangular cunt.
    She had to learn for diversion
    A posterior perversion
For no one could fit her in front.

The soldier became so uncouth,
When his cock was shot off in his youth.
    He screwed with his nose
    And his fingers and toes
And he came through a hole in his tooth.

———————————

A rapturous young fellatrix
One day was at work on five pricks.
    With an unholy cry
    She whipped out her glass eye.
And yelled, "Tell the boys I can take six!"

A foolhardy midget named Fisher
Stuck his wong in a fat lady's fissure.
    Her labial snap
    Caught him in a trap
Now they're fishing the fissure for Fisher.

———————

At nudist camps, signs aren't so rare
Telling members, "Of midgets, beware!"
    For they make members weep
    For they just cannot keep
Their noses out of private affairs.

The front of the young girl oft got rises
For her breasts were of two different sizes.
    One was so small
    It was nothing at all,
But the other was huge and won prizes.

———————————

A young man whose sight was myopic
Shied away from all sex, as a topic.
    So poor were his eyes
    That despite its great size
His penis appeared microscopic.

The cock of a fellow named Randall
Shot sparks like a big Roman candle.
    He was much in demand
    For the colors were grand,
But the girls found him to hot to handle.

There once was a eunuch of Roylem
Took two eggs to the cook and said, "Boil 'em.
    I'll sling them beneath
    My inadequate sheath,
And slip into the harem and foil 'em."

There was a young lady from Munich
Who was had in the park by a eunuch.
    In a moment of passion
    He shot her a ration
From a squirt-gun concealed 'neath his tunic.

A girl making love with Joe Poole
Felt his passion grow suddenly cool.
    But no lack of affection
    Reduced his erection—
But his zipper had closed on his tool.

A young traveler in Tahiti,
Went for a nude swim with his sweetie.
    But as he pursued her
    A huge barracuda
Bit off his erect masculinity.

———————

On a wanton young wife name of Zelda
Her husband a chastity belt welded.
    She tried picking the lock
    With the gardener's cock
And the next thing he knew, he was gelded.

4

REVOLTING RACIAL
AND ETHNIC LIMERICKS

There is a young nurse in Japan
Who lifts men by their pricks to the pan.
    This trick of jujitsu
    Has castrated a few,
But it's made others more of a man.

There was a young Polack named Bob
Who explained to his friends with a sob,
    "I had a huge phallus
     Till the night I goosed Alice,
And she bit off my shank at the knob."

———————————

There was a Norwegian named Knute
Who suffered from warts on his root.
    He put acid on these
     And now, when he pees,
He must finger his prick like a flute.

An Italian man named Marini
Found he had a dozen little bambini.
    He said, "If I thought,
    Thata my sauce was so hot,
I'da never put inna my weenie."

———————

There once was a handsome Croatian
Who was the luckiest man in creation.
    For his job was the treat
    Teaching the Commie elite
The art of erotic copulation.

There was an old midwife in Gaul
Who had hardly no business at all.
    She cried, "Hell and damnation!
    There's no procreation—
God made the French penis too small!"

———————————

A malicious harlot from Bogota,
Constructed an erotic pagoda,
    And on all the walls,
    She hung all the balls
And the tools of the fools who bestrode her.

There once was a rich WASPish bitch
Who owned a gold dildo, the which,
    She would use with delight
    Far into the night,
Scratching her avaricious itch.

————————

In Poland there once was a lass,
Who'd been born with a triangular ass.
    The men came in herds,
    To see her drop turds,
Each a perfect pyramidal mass.

There was a young Frenchman from Nantes
Who all morals and laws he did flaunt,
    For he screwed all his dozens,
    Of nieces and cousins,
In addition, of course, to his aunt.

———————————

A young Polish girl gained great fame,
Through her unusual sexual games.
    She was great fun to lay,
    For her rectum would play,
Lively polkas, then call you bad names.

A WOP lawyer who filed a writ,
Nearly gave the poor judge a big fit.
    When reproved for a fart,
     He said, with a start,
"Whenever I break wind, I shit."

———————————

A young Polish peasant from Gorsk,
Fell madly in love with his horse.
    Said his wife, "You rapscallion,
     That horse is a stallion—
And sodomy's grounds for divorce."

A horny young male Eskimo
Couldn't come by just rubbing a nose.
    He slipped out of his hut
      To search for a white slut
Who knew how to suck and to blow.

———————

A prudish WASP girl in New York
Plugged up her cunt with a cork.
    A woodpecker or two,
      Made the grade, it is true,
But she totally baffled the stork.

An Italian girl named Astaire
Was totally covered by hair.
    But the boys all got kicks
    From probing with pricks,
For her pussy could be anywhere.

———————

Said the old whore to the arrogant Fong,
"You're rude and you're utterly wrong,
    To say my vagina
    Is the largest in China,
Just because of your puny, thin dong."

The prim lady Bostonian
Had been raised to think sex was a sin.
  But when she was tight
  Fornication seemed right
So she lunched every day on straight gin.

A Russian young lady of fashion,
Had oodles and oodles of passion.
  To her lovers she said,
  As they'd climb into bed,
"Here's one thing those Commies can't ration."

The Wop girl with features cherubic
Had a monstrous area pubic.
    When asked about her size
    She replied with surprise,
"Are you asking 'bout square feet, or cubic?"

———————————

An Irishman born in Connaught
Had a penis incredibly short.
    His bride, shocked, said,
    When they climbed into bed,
"That isn't a prick, it's a wart."

5

LEWD SENIOR CITIZEN LIMERICKS

A painted and padded old wench
Oft claimed not to know what they meant.
    When men asked her her age,
    She'd exclaim in great rage,
"My age is the age of consent!"

A desperate spinster named Clare
Once knelt in the moonlight all bare
    And prayed to her God
    "Take me here on the sod."
Then a passerby answered her prayer.

The wizened old maid from Madras
Bragged of her magnificent ass;
    But it was not rounded and pink,
    As she hoped people would think—
It was gray, had long ears, and ate grass.

A king sadly said to his Queen,
"In parts you have grown far from lean."
    She said, "I don't give a damn,
    You always craved beef and ham."
He sneered, "That's a thought most obscene."

———————

There was an old lady of Asia
Who had an odd kind of amnesia.
    She'd forget that her cunt
    Was located in front,
Which deprived her of most of her pleasure.

Said a worldly old maid named Noreen,
"I prefer a man of eighteen,
    His pecker's more stiff,
    When it thrusts in my quiff,
And he screws in a manner obscene."

———————

A skinny old maid from Sheboygan
Wed a short-peckered son-of-a-gun.
    She said, "I don't care
    If there isn't much there.
God knows it is better than none."

There was a young lady, Miss Rockinham,
Who'd accept any cocks without pickin' 'em.
    Then she'd kneel on the sod,
     And pray to her God
To lengthen and strengthen and thicken them.

The old woman hopped on for a ride,
And they humped—till he suddenly died.
    His wife, for a week,
     Sat on his stiff peak,
And bounced up and down as she cried.

There was an old maid name of May
Who was strolling one day by the bay.
    She was seized by a man
    Who raped her and ran.
Now she goes to the bay every day.

————————

There was a crass whore in Berlin
Who was fucked by an elderly Finn.
    He attacked her with zest
    Asking, "Am I the best?"
Her reply: "Hey, Pop, is it in?"

Said an old maid one fondly remembers,
"Now my days are quite clearly Septembers.
    All my fires have burned low,
    I'll admit that it's so,
But you still might have fun in the embers."

———————

A poor widow found herself in great need.
She had nothing to eat but some seeds.
    Soon huge tufts of grass
    Sprouted out of her ass
And her cunt was all covered with weeds.

There was an old harlot named Lofton,
Who was screwed amazingly often.
    At sex she was tested.
    She never was rested,
Until she was screwed in her coffin.

———————————

A horny soldier from Fort Blaney,
Seduced an old maid named Miss Faney.
    When his friends, they did jeer,
    That she was old and so queer,
He replied, "But the day was so rainy!"

6

APPALLING ANIMAL LIMERICKS

A besotted wench had an affair
With a fellow all covered with hair.
    Then she picked up his hat
      And realized that
She'd been had by Smokey the Bear.

There was an old hermit of Ware
Who had an affair with a bear.
    He explained, "I don't mind,
    For she's gentle and kind,
But I wish she had slightly less hair."

—————————

A young girl on a trip to the equator,
Was fucked by an old alligator.
    No one ever knew
    How she relished that screw,
For after he fucked her, he ate her.

A disgusting young man named McGill
Made his neighbors exceedingly ill.
    When they learned of his habits
    Involving white rabbits
And a bird with a flexible bill.

———————

There was a farmer named Osteen
Who was screwing a milking machine.
    On the thirty-fifth stroke
    The goddamn thing broke
And beat his balls into whipped cream.

One night a zookeeper named Rawls
Fell asleep while he washed some cage walls.
    He was jolted awake
    When a very large snake
Was swallowing both of his balls.

———————————

There was a young lady of Worcester
Who dreamt that a rooster had seduced her.
    She woke with a scream
    But 'twas only a dream—
A bump in the mattress had goosed her.

There was a young fellow from Kent
Who had a peculiar bent
    He collected the turds
    Of various birds
And had them for lunch during Lent.

———————————

A stableman's daughter named Prentiss
Is morally *non compos mentis.*
    She seduces her dad,
    And when dad can't be had,
Uses horses in loco parentis.

A drunken old woman named Rupps
Confessed one night in her cups,
    "My life's worst folly,
     Was fucking my collie—
But I got a nice price for the pups."

———————————

There was a young lady named Schneider,
Who had an ungodly passion for spiders.
    She found a strange bliss,
     In the sound of her piss,
As it strained through the cobwebs inside her.

There was a young farm girl named Sutton,
Who said, as she carved up the mutton,
    "My father preferred,
    Screwing sheep from the herd,
This is one of his children I'm cuttin'."

—————————

The cost of bordellos was steep,
And the horny old Scot was so cheap,
    That when he wanted to screw,
    There was nothing to do,
But take out his passion on sheep.

A wanton young woman named Lake,
Fell so perversely in love with her snake,
    That she wished the boa
    Could shoot spermatozoa,
So remarkable offspring they'd make.

———————————

A zookeeper in lovely Capri,
Screwed a baboon by the sea.
    The results were most horrid,
    All ass and no forehead,
Four balls and a purple goatee.

A hot-blooded Scot from Glasgow
Didn't care where he buried his prow.
    In one day he screwed,
    Four whores and a ewe,
Then ended by fucking a sow.

A ranch hand, from years in the saddle,
Had a penis as flat as a paddle.
    It was his rotten luck,
    That no sheep could he fuck.
He could only have sex with the cattle.

There was a young farmer named Rule
Who had a long and incredible tool.
    He could use it to plow,
     Or to screw a young cow,
Or just as a cue stick at pool.

'Tis reported the Prince Montezuma
Once had an affair with a puma.
    The puma in play
     Clawed both balls away,
An example of animal humor.

7

MORTIFYING
MASTURBATION LIMERICKS

There was a young man of Montrose
Who could diddle himself with his toes.
    He did it so neat
    He fell in love with his feet
And christened them Agnes and Rose.

A lusty young woodsman of Maine
For years with no woman had lain.
    But he found sublimation
    At a high elevation
In the crotch of a pine—God, the pain!

———————

There was a young swimmer named Chad
Who one night dreamt that he was a shad.
    He dreamt he was spawning
    And then, the next morning,
He saw on the sheets that he had.

There was a young man from Green Bay
Who fashioned a cunt out of clay.
    But the heat of his prick
    Turned it into a brick
And chafed all his foreskin away.

A squeamish young fellow named Brand
Thought caressing his penis was grand.
    But he viewed with distaste
    The gelatinous paste
That it left in the palm of his hand.

There was an old maid name of Croft,
Who played with herself in a loft,
    Having reasoned that candles
    Could never cause scandals,
Besides which, they did not go soft.

———————————

A geneticist whose name was Ralph
Used a test tube to play with himself.
    And when he was done,
    He labeled it, "Son."
And filed him away on the shelf.

An agreeable girl named Miss Doves
Likes to jack off the young men she loves.
    She will use her bare fist
    If the fellows insist,
But she really prefers to wear gloves.

———————————

A certain young fellow named Dick
Liked to feel a girl's hand on his prick.
    He taught them to fool
    The right way with his tool,
Till the cream shot out nice and thick.

A timid young woman named Grace
Refused adamantly to place
    Her hand on a cock
    When it turned hard as rock,
For fear it would explode in her face.

———————————

A naive young boy from farm land
Was told that fucking was grand.
    But at his first trial,
    He said with a smile,
"I've had the same feeling by hand."

There was a young lady named Alice
Who used dynamite for a phallus.
    They found her vagina
    In North Carolina
And the rest of her rained down on Dallas.

———————

A proper young lady from Wheeling
Oft professed to lack sexual feeling.
    But a cynic named Boris
    Just touched her clitoris
And she had to be scraped off the ceiling.

Masturbation, according to Freud
Is a very good thing to avoid.
    If practiced each day,
    Your balls will decay
To the size of a small adenoid.

There was a young virgin named Alice
Who thought of her cunt as a chalice.
    One night, sleeping nude
    She awoke feeling lewd
And found in her chalice, a phallus.

A young lady who suffered a hernia,
Said to her fresh doctor, "God darn ya,
    When inspecting my middle,
     You'd better not fiddle,
With matters that do not concern ya."

———————

While on a hunting vacation
The lodge members tried new recreation
    Till their cabin was teemin'
     With buckets of semen
From hot mutual masturbation.

8

RAUNCHY SEX LIMERICKS

A pretty young maiden of France
Decided she'd once take a chance
    She let herself go
    For an hour or so
And now all of her sisters are aunts.

"It's time," said a hooker, Miss Loring,
"That new avenues, I go exploring.
    This street corner jazz
    Is a pain in the ass,
And the men you meet whoring are boring."

The lustful young wife was a rover
Who adulterously told men who drove her
    To cry, when they came,
    "Oh, my, what a shame,
We'll have to start up all over!"

There's a starlet who's still in her teens,
Who's adept at removing her jeans.
    And in x-rated flicks
    So accomplished with pricks
That she steals all the pictures' obscene.

Said the female exec, to her beau,
"I've developed a pragmatic credo.
    I support ERA
    But there's times when I stray,
And the lib I support is libido."

A maid in the land of Aloha
Got laid in the prow of a proa.
    And as the island stud sneezed
    The maid, not displeased
Cried, "Come on, let's do it Samoa."

———————————

Under the stars waxed a lecher most heinous.
To the girl, "Don't let morals restrain us.
    Though I've made a career,
    Out of Venus, my dear,
I am tempted to switch to Uranus."

There was a young coed from Norwood
Whose ways were provokingly forward.
    Said her mother, "My dear,
    You wiggle, I fear,
Your posterior the way that a whore would."

———————————

There was a young coed at Kent
Who said that she knew what it meant
    When studs asked her to dine
    Upon lobster and wine.
She knew. Oh, she knew. But she went!

There was a young girl from Penn State
Who stuttered when out on a date.
　　By the time she cried, "S-s-s-stop!"
　　Or called for a c-c-c-cop,
It was often a wee bit too late.

———————

"I'll tell," smiled frat chairman Mose,
"Why Hatty's the ball date I chose.
　　She's as cheerfully free,
　　As the wind o'er the sea,
And besides, like the wind, Hatty blows."

At Wellesley, Vassar, and Smith
A common and recurring myth
    That a masculine member
    Helps students remember
Was found to lack substance or pith.

A clever commercial female
Had prices tattooed on her tail.
    And on that same behind,
    For the sake of the blind,
Was the same information in Braille.

There was a young lady from Plain View
Whose boyfriend said, "May I explore you?"
    She replied to the chap,
    "I will draw you a map,
Where others have been to before you."

A shapely young lady named Fern
Puts out and is paid in return.
    "And my earnings," she said,
    "I conceal in my bed,
Since the ads say to save where you earn."

Three girls and a captain named Hanson
Had a very rough sailing vacation.
    The ladies got tough
    And swam off in a huff.
The man was the bone of contention.

———————————

A beach boy who loved to have fun
Kept screwing a girl in the sun.
    While his ass, being bare,
    Cooked to medium rare,
The girl kept exclaiming, "Well done."

A sneaky young bachelor named Lodge,
Had seat belts installed in his Dodge.
    Once a broad was strapped in
    They could commit sin
Without even leaving the garage.

———————

With Robert, her boyfriend, Miss Cobb
Would nod when engaged in a job.
    It was wrongfully said
    She was bobbing her head,
When she really was heading her Bob.

There was a young lady who said,
As her bridegroom got into the bed,
    "I'm tired of this stunt,
    That they do with my cunt,
You can enter my bottom instead."

———————————

There was a young knight name of Lancelot,
On whom women all looked askance a lot.
    Whenever he'd pass,
    Any maiden or lass,
The front of his pants would advance a lot.

There once was a Senator Mark,
Who encountered a cunt in the dark.
    He said, "Now, by thunder,
     It's a national treasure,
I declare this a national park."

———————

There was a young girl whose frigidity,
Approached cataleptic rigidity.
    Till you gave her a drink,
     And she would quickly sink,
In a state of complaisant liquidity.

There was a young lady from Wheeling
Who was out in the garden a-kneeling.
    When by some strange chance
    She got ants in her pants,
And invented Virginia reeling.

———————

A handsome young pro name of Dennis
Made good money teaching girls tennis.
    But the game he played best
    Far more than the rest,
Was played with two balls and a penis.

The mathematician Von Blecks
Devised an equation for sex,
    Having proved a good fuck
    Isn't patience or luck,
But a function of y over x.

———————

There was a young lady named Smith
Whose virtue was largely a myth.
    She said, "Try as I can,
    I can't find a man,
Who it's fun to be virtuous with."

A young baseball groupie named Glenda
Was the home-team's biggest rooter and friend.
    But for her the big league
    Never held the intrigue
Of a bat with two balls at the end.

———————

There was a young goddess, a Venus
Who was obsessed with her lover's big penis.
    She loved pubic hair
    And balls that were bare,
And she loved jacking him off into Kleenex.

There was a young parson named Gary
Who was morbidly anxious to marry.
    But he found the defection,
     Of any erection,
A difficult problem to parry.

A vigorous fellow named Burt
Was attracted by every new skirt.
    Oh, it wasn't their minds
    But their rounded behinds
That excited this loveable flirt.

There was a young fellow named Hiss
Whose sex life was strangely amiss.
    With the most beautiful Venus
    His recalcitrant penis
Would never do better than t
               h
                 i
                   s.

There was a young lady named Rose
Who'd occasionally straddle a hose,
    And parade about squirting
    And spouting and spurting,
Pretending she pissed like her beau.

There was a young lady named Rose,
With erogenous zones in her toes.
    She remained onanistic
    Till a foot-fetichistic
Young man became one of her beaux.

––––––––––––––

An innocent coed, Miss Muldow
Cooed, "Oh my, I don't even know how."
    But her professor caught her
    And so thoroughly taught her,
She takes on men in threesomes now.

There once was a sensitive bride,
Who ran when the groom she espied.
    When she looked at his swiver,
    She started to quiver,
But when he got it in, well, she sighed.

A young man of morals inferior
Was groping a lady's posterior.
    He said, "Say, my pet,
    Your panties are wet."
"Sorry, sir, that's my interior!"

There was a pianist named Liszt
Who played with one hand while he pissed.
    But as he grew older,
    His technique grew bolder,
And in concert jacked off with his fist.

There was a young lady named Tucker
Who jerked off with a tart lemon sucker.
    The candy got stuck
    And now she can't fuck
Because her vagina did pucker.

There once was a couple named Kelly
Who had to live belly to belly,
    Because once in their haste
    They used library paste
Instead of petroleum jelly.

———————

A man who picnicked with a lass
Ended up making love in the grass.
    But the heat of the sun
    Spoiled most of his fun
By burning the skin of his ass.

A young lady wore, one late fall,
A newspaper dress to a Halloween Ball.
  The dress caught on fire
  And burned her entire
Front page, sporting section and all.

———————————

A horny old trucker named Van Dam
Got a blow job while driving his tandem.
  Just as he shot his load,
  The truck jumped off the road.
And scattered their bodies at random.

A young lady golfer named Duff
Had a lovely, luxuriant muff.
    In his haste to get in her
    One eager beginner
Lost both of his balls in the rough.

———————

The buxom young chorus girl in Reno,
Lost all her bucks playing Keno.
    But then she turned bawdy,
    And married a Saudi,
And now she owns the casino.

Exxon, Standard Oil and Shell
Formed a big world-wide pussy cartel.
    Till it took scads of money
     For even one taste of honey
A poor man could not get a smell.

———————————

A shiftless young fellow named Kent
Had his wife fuck the landlord for rent.
    But as she grew older
     The landlord grew colder
And now they live out in a tent.

There was a young girl name of Dale
Who put her ass up for sale.
    For a twenty buck ante,
    You could feel her fanny,
And a fifty would get you real tail.

———————

A husband who craved to be sterile
Because of the pregnancy peril
    Said, "I've thought of vasectomy
    But my wife then might hector me,
And threaten divorce when we quarrel."

The young lady received an affrontage
When her contractor took an advantage.
    Said the County Surveyor,
     "Of course, you must pay her,
You've altered the line of her frontage."

———————————

The he-man strode into her office,
Ripped off her pants, then took off his.
    He displayed his huge rod—
    The difference, by God—
Between what a he-man and a boy is.

There was a young lady named Flo
Whose lover pulled out way too slow.
    So they tried it all night
    Till he got it just right.
Well, practice makes pregnant, you know.

———————————

There was a young man most forlorn
Whose parents wished he'd never been born.
    For he wouldn't have been
    If his father had seen
That the end of the rubber was torn.

A girl lay with her beau by the fire
Then succumbed to her lover's desire.
    She moaned, "That's a sin
    But now that it's in,
Could you shove it a few inches higher."

———————

A philanthropist name of Simon
Launched a nationwide search for a hymen.
    But they found every girl
    Had relinquished that pearl
In exchange for a jewel or some stipend.

No one can tell about Myrtle
Whether she's sterile or fertile.
    If anyone tries
    To tickle her thighs
She closes them tight like a turtle.

———————

There was a young girl from Hoboken
Who claimed that her hymen was broken
    From riding a bike
    On a cobblestone pike,
But it really was broken from pokin'.

A devout young lady most fair,
Was having her first love affair.
    As she climbed into bed
    She reverently said,
"I wish to be opened with prayer."

———————————

There was a young lady named Drew
Whose cherry a chap had got through
    Which she told to her mother
    Who fixed her another
Out of rubber and red ink and glue.

There was a young tease name of Linda
Who'd flash her bare charms out the window.
    But she'd slam her legs shut
    The contemptible slut
Whenever you tried to climb inda.

———————

There was a young virgin most rude
Whose tricks, though exciting, were viewed
    With distrust by the males
    For she'd fondle their rails
But never would let them intrude.

On a maiden a man once begat,
Male triplets named Nat, Pat and Tat.
    It was fun in the breeding,
     But hell in the feeding.
She hadn't a spare tit for Tat.

———————————

When asked to do something salacious
She answered, "Of course not! Good gracious!"
    But the sight of his tool,
     So induced her to drool,
That her view, in the end, was fellatious.

"It's my code," said a mailman named Drew,
"To unzip, then deliver a screw.
    If virgins, when nervous,
    Resist postal service,
I explain that the male must go through."

———————————

While the bill was debated, Miss Snyder
Had a senator thrusting inside her.
    To a knock on the door,
    He replied from the floor,
"Go away, I'm inserting a rider."

Said a hooker on Wall Street named Bond,
"I've a trick of which clients are fond.
    When I've hairsprayed some gold,
    Where my labia fold,
I'm a gilt-edged negotiable blonde."

————————

Call the study of figures statistics,
And the study of language, linguistics,
    But it's clear that one errs,
    When one loosely avers
That the study of balling's ballistics.

In the farm belt, a hooker named Blum,
Who's the favorite floozy of some,
    Takes her teeth out in bed,
    To administer head,
Since her tricks love it, by gum!

———————————

A quick-witted art critic in Soho,
Accosted a fortnight ago,
    Is alleged to have quipped,
    When a flasher unzipped,
"Your exhibit's well hung, sir. Good show!"

The beaver of hot-pantied Pearl
Incredibly just didn't curl.
    Whén a hot-handed date
    Said, "Your twat hair's so straight!"
She suggested he give it a whirl.

Once bedded, your feminist miss,
Is likely to say, with a hiss,
    "By God, all us sisters,
    Would kick out all you misters,
If we didn't need *that* to do *this!*"

A real estate man's imperfections,
As a lover caused female rejections.
    "I'm deflated," he moaned.
    "They're erogenous zoned,
But only for high-rise erections."

———————————

There was a young man from Sioux Falls
Renowned in vaudeville halls.
    His favorite trick,
    Was to stand on his prick
And then slide off the stage on his balls.

Said the wife, "My husband's a creep,
I'm so tired and pissed I could weep.
    For my husband demands,
     To hold a tit in each hand,
Then the bastard walks 'round in his sleep."

———————

There was a young girl name of Bass
Who had absolutely no class.
    Her idea to please,
     Was to get on her knees
So a prick could be shoved up her ass.

A horny young girl in a mansion,
Got laid three times by a man most handsome.
    When she cried out for more,
    There came a groan from the floor,
The man said, "I'm Simpson, not Samson."

———————

An acrobatic young man with blond hair
Was fucking a girl on the stair.
    The bannister broke
    But he doubled his stroke
And finished her off in mid-air.

In the Garden of Eden lay Adam,
Complacently stroking his madam.
    He chuckled with mirth,
    For in all of the earth,
There were only two tits, and he had 'em!

————————

Her curvacious young aunt told her this:
"Making love in the hay is great bliss.
    For it tickles my bun
    And helps me to come
WHEN COMFORTABLY LYING LIKE THIS

A dentist who divorced his old crone
Began seeing patients alone.
    In a fit of depravity
    He filled the wrong cavity
And soon found that his practice had grown.

———————————

His wife had a nice little cunt;
It was hairy, and soft, and in front.
    And with this she'd fuck him
    Though sometimes she'd suck him
A charming, if commonplace, stunt.

A naive but shapely hygenist
Abhored the horny old dentist.
    To make his conquest easier
    He gave her anesthesia
Then screwed her, *non compos mentis*.

Of his face the girl thought not so much,
But then, at the very first touch
    Her attitude shifted.
    He was terribly gifted
At licking, and sucking, and such.

A nymphet who liked to run free,
Used to perch like a bird in a tree.
    Any one who came there
    Saw her asshole was bare
And so was her C-U-N-T.

———————————

A proper WASP lawyer named Fife,
Had a marriage just filled with great strife
    For he thought a perdition
    Every sexual position
But lying on top of his wife.

A bird watching man name of Hanks
Was stalking up a river bank.
In the waist high rye grass
He stepped right on an ass
Then heard a young girl call out, "Thanks!"

———————

There was a young fellow of Kent
Whose prick was so long that it bent.
So to save himself trouble
He put it in double
And instead of coming, he went.

If you talk about actions immoral,
Then you'll have to award a big laurel
    To a **WAVE** on the sea
    Who took men in threes—
One fore, one aft, and one oral.

———————

There was a young fellow from Florida,
Who liked a friend's wife, so he borrowed her.
    When they climbed into the sack,
    He cried out, "Alack!
This isn't a cunt, it's a corridor!"

A gorgeous young woman named Sweeney,
Was a cock teasing bitch, a true meanie.
     The hatch of her snatch,
     Had a latch that would catch.
She could only be screwed by Houdini.

———————————

Said a man who was known for his larks,
"I like sex inside, not in parks,
     For you feel more at ease,
     And your ass doesn't freeze,
And bystanders don't make snide remarks."

A fencing instructor named Fisk
At sex was too terribly brisk.
　　So fast was his action
　　That his lover's contractions,
Foreshortened his foil to a disk.

───────────

A young circus man name of Dick
Perfected a most wonderful trick.
　　With a safe for protection
　　He'd get an erection
And then balance himself on his prick.

9

SIMPLY DISGUSTING

She wasn't what one would call pretty.
All the other girls offered her pity;
    So nobody guessed
    That her syphillis test
Panicked half the men in the city.

A sperm faced, alack and forsooth,
His moment of sexual truth.
    He's expected to fall
    On a womb's spongy wall
But was dashed to his death on a tooth.

———————————

A mortician's young daughter named Maddie
Told an eager, virginial laddie,
    "If you do what I say,
    We can have a great lay,
Since I've buried more stiffs than my daddy."

The girl was beset with hysteria,
For she thought she'd come down with malaria.
    But the family doc
    Remarked, to her shock,
"It's crabs in the vaginal area."

There was a young lady named Alice
Who purchased a hard rubber phallus.
    Since she learned its perfections
    She shuns doctor's inspections—
It is *such* an odd place for a callus.

A morbid young woman named Jean
Was known as the Masochist Queen.
    She used thistles and cactus
     In her sadistic practice,
In a manner both odd and obscene.

An unfortunate hooker from Summit
Everytime she got laid, had to vomit.
    When her man got a bone
     She turned over and moaned,
"Give it here," she would say, "let me gum it."

An unfortunate fellow named Chase
Had an ass that was quite out of place.
    It caused consternation,
    When an investigation
Showed that he shit through his face.

An untutored rural young Texan,
Couldn't tell his behind from a hole in
    That good Texas ground,
    Till the day that he found,
That oil wouldn't come out of his colon.

There was a most vicious harlot
Who wished she had teeth in her twat.
    "For just think," said she,
    "How nice it would be,
To cut and mount all the pricks I have had."

———————

There once was a pretty young miss,
Who enjoyed watching her lover piss.
    She made him drink beer,
    By the quart, all the year,
And this Lager assured her of bliss.

A disgusting harlot, Louise,
Had cunt-hair that hung down to her knees
    Till the crabs in her twat
    Tied the hair in a knot,
And constructed a flying trapeze.

———————————

A buxom strip dancer named Jane
Wore a costume of thin cellophane.
    When asked why she wore it,
    She said, "I abhor it,
But my cunt juice would spatter like rain."

There was a young lady from China
Who mistook for her mouth, her vagina.
    Her clitoris huge
    She covered with rouge
And lipsticked her labia minor.

———————————

There was a young girl from Connecticut
Who didn't care much about etiquette.
    Whenever she was able,
    She'd piss on the table
And mop off her cunt with her petticoat.

A filthy young lady named Daisy
Was really infernally lazy.
    She hadn't the time
    To wipe her behind,
And the stench of it drove her men crazy.

———————

A milkmaid there was, with a stutter,
Who was lonely and wanted a futter.
    She had no where to turn,
    So she diddled a churn,
And managed to come with the butter.

A widow whose singular vice
Was to keep her late husband on ice
    Said, "It's been hard since I lost him—
    I'll never defrost him!
Cold comfort, but cheap at the price."

———————

A sheriff from Bennington Junction
Whose organ had long ceased to function
    Deceived his good wife
    For the rest of her life
With the aid of his trusty wood truncheon.

There was a young man most obscene
Who invented a fucking machine.
    Concave or convex
    It would fit either sex,
With attachments for those in between.

———————

A woman at cruise on the sea,
Who said, "God, how it hurts me to pee."
    "I see," said the doc
    "That accounts for the pox,
Of the captain, the first mate, and me."

The young lady said to old Chester,
When he broke in her room to molest her,
    "I think that you'll find,
    That you'd best change your mind,
For with herpes my pussy does fester."

———————————

The streetwalker said to the hick,
"I refuse to suck farmers' boys' dicks.
    I really don't mind
    The hay dust and the grime
But the smell of your balls makes me sick."

The young whore was such a crass shrew
She filled her vagina with glue.
    She said with a grin,
    "If they pay to get in,
They'll pay to get out of it, too."

————————

Said a woman pushing two baby carriages
"What a strange twist of fate, marriage is.
    When you stop to think
    That I've thrown in the drink
Five abortions and five miscarriages."

There was a young Royal Marine,
Who tried to fart "God Save the Queen."
    When he reached the soprano,
    Out came the guano
And his britches weren't fit to be seen.

———————

There was a young Scotsman from Troon,
Who farted and filled a balloon.
    The gas drove it so high
    That it soared through the sky
And stank out the Man in the Moon.

There was a young wife of Bill Dexter,
Whose husband exceedingly vexed her.
    In bed, when they'd start,
    He'd invariably fart
With a blast that would nearly unsex her.

———————————

There was a young student named Harter
Who achieved great reknown as a farter.
    His deafening reports
    At spectator sports
Made him in much demand as a starter.

There was a young man name of Brewster,
Who said to his wife, as he goosed her,
    "It used to be grand,
    But now look at my hand!
You aren't wiping clean as you used to."

There was a young man from Brighton,
Who thought he'd at last found a tight one.
    He said, "Oh, my love,
    It fits like a glove."
Said she, "But you're not in the right one."

There was an old man in Bogota,
Who would not pay a whore what he owed her.
    She didn't curse, did not swear.
    She just climbed on a chair,
And pissed in his whiskey-and-soda.

———————————

A toothsome young starlet named Smart
Was asked to display oral art
    As the price for the role.
    She complied, met his goal.
And then sank her teeth in the part.

The young woman's masturbational style,
Is distinguished by Frenchified guile:
    She uses a wiener—
    It's safer and cleaner—
She's become a confirmed Frankophile!

———————

A crab working hookers in Natchez,
Takes refuge, when one of them scratches,
    In her nook, for a nap,
    For the shrewd little chap,
Finds he's safest when sleeping in snatches.

"I regret," she announced with a smile,
"That our music must wait for a while.
    I would love a duet,
    But I can't join you yet,
Because ragtime was never my style."

———————

There was an old miser named Dave
Who kept a dead whore in his cave.
    He said, "I'm perverse,
    As a lay, it's the worst,
But think of the money I save!"

A mortician who practiced in Fife
Made love to the corpse of his wife.
    "How could I know, Judge?
     She was cold and did not budge—
Just the same as she acted in life."

———————————

A prostitute's perfect condition
Was a tribute to sperm as nutrition.
    Her remarkable diet—
     She urged all to try it—
Was solely her clients' emission.

While screwing one night, this big schmuck,
Got nipples in his ear stuck.
    Then, his thumb up her bun
    He heard himself come,
Thus inventing the radio fuck.

———————————

A surly old man, most malicious
Liked his sex perverse and vicious.
    He fucked two of his nieces
    Then cut them to pieces
And cooked up a stew most delicious.

The French Legionnaires were fighters determined
But their sex lives were those of mean vermin.
    When in from patrol
    They'd screw any hole
That would possibly let any sperm in.

———————

There was a young lady named Inge
Who went on a popsicle binge.
    I won't breathe a word
    Of what really occurred,
But her cunt has a damp, sticky fringe.

A horny young lady from France,
Said yes every time she had the chance.
    But she thought it was crude
    To make love in the nude
So she always went home with wet pants.

———————

A clumsy young virgin named Fred
Took a patient old hooker to bed.
    She let him fiddle awhile
    Then pointed out with a smile,
"You've got it all in but the head."

A lady tourist supping in Peru,
Found an elephant's cock in her stew.
    Said the waiter, "Don't shout!
    Please don't wave it about,
Or the women will all want one, too."

––––––––––––––––

There was a drunk actor from Stockton
Who told the black girl, "You're a tight one."
    She replied, "'Pon my soul,
    You're in the wrong hole.
There's plenty of room in the right one!"

He seduced her and started to rub her,
But, frustrated, was heard to mutter,
   "If your feminine glands,
    Don't respond to my hands,
I'm afraid I shall have to use butter."

A sexy young girl from old Ipswich
Had a nearly intolerable crotch itch.
   Till her neighbor's son, Jack
    Laid her flat on her back
And united the organs they pissed with.

A maiden who lived in Virginny,
Had a cunt that could bark, neigh, and whinny
    The hunting set chased her,
    But then they replaced her,
When the pitch of her organ went tinny.

———————

The young stud got blasted on coke
Then picked up a girl for a poke.
    He stripped off her pants,
    Fucked her into a trance,
Then shit in her shoes for a joke.

A self-deceived woman named Brook
Coyly referred to her cunt as a "nook."
　　But it was really so wide
　　You could curl up inside
With a big easy chair and a book.

———————————

A young Cajun lady from Natchez,
Was unfortunately born with two snatches.
　　She often cursed, "Shit!
　　I'd give up both my tits,
For a man with equipment that matches."

A man found his young maiden bride
Had a cunt that was twelve inches wide.
    The groom said, "To fuck it,
     I need a prick like a bucket.
To keep me from falling inside."

A young man in chemistry class
Coated his testes with brass.
    When they jangled together
     In wet, stormy weather,
Lightning shot out of his ass.

There was a young girl from Madrid,
Who learned she was having a kid.
    By holding her water,
     For a month and a quarter,
She drowned the poor infant, she did.

———————————

A lovesick skydiver named Sherm
Bailed out with his prick long and firm.
    Two jerks plus a spasm,
     Produced an orgasm,
And he spelled out, "I love you" in sperm.